HEAVEN ON EARTH

THE ULTIMATE GUIDE TO LIVING AN EVOLVED LIFE

By Iain Grae and Emily Wilson

WHO IS THIS FOR?

Are you ready to unleash the courage, passion and drive to your full potential? To know your purpose? To dream bigger than ever before? Are you ready to claim your birthright?

This book is designed to create a blueprint that will attract the life you've longed for. You can expect to gain massive clarity and bring the life you've always dreamed about into your reality. Get ready to stretch your imagination of what is possible as you create your story, your Heaven on Earth.

The simple and elegant design of this blueprint holds a key vibration to bring things from the fifth dimension into the third dimensional reality. This vibration leverages the 14 fundamental laws of creation. It is designed so that you don't have to understand all the science or mysticism behind it. *My Heaven on Earth* is the book that allows anyone with imagination, faith and courage to realize their true power.

Every person on the planet has the ability to create their own Heaven on Earth. This book is designed to do just that.

While there may be references to great spiritual teachers, this book transcends any single religion and will aid anyone in leveraging deeper spiritual truths to create the material world of Heaven on Earth.

It is my understanding that there are many people on earth right now who are experiencing unnecessary suffering. It may be in their relationships with friends, family or at work. It may be in their physical or mental health. It may be in finances where money seems to be elusive. It may be that life has become anything less than the blissful adventure it is supposed to be. It may be that the connection to the divine life force that flows through one is ready to be expanded and brought to the next level. It may be all of these.

This book is intended to help anyone in realizing the vision of Heaven on Earth that they hold in their heart and to manifest it. This may be to build a business empire, to experience love in all of their relationships, to have excellent health, to feel empowered and free or to gain access to a higher power and realize the gifts that lie within. As one completes this book, the clarity of one's purpose and how to get there is revealed in a dynamic, intentional and actionable way.

"The kingdom of Heaven on Earth is within you."
-    *Jesus Christ*

Evolved Life Publishing

Evolved Life
6801 Collins Ave
Miami Beach, Florida 33141
United States
+1 (213) 640-9395
live@evolvedlife.com

ABOUT IAIN GRAE

At 13 years old, after being inspired by several books including *The Mental Edge*, *Think & Grow Rich* and *As a Man Thinketh*, I created my first working model of *My Heaven on Earth*. What was to come next was beyond explanation. At the time, I wasn't a great student, a few years earlier I was in remedial gym and reading. I had an interesting relationship with the other kids, with one pegging me in the face with football while I was staring off into nature wondering how I would ever fit in to the new school I was attending. I remember my friend's mother laughing hysterically when I shared the list of colleges I planned on attending. It appeared as if my ability to be successful in life was far from likely. The thing that no one knew was that I already had my first model of my Heaven on Earth blueprint. This model was already working very successfully in my motocross racing career.

By using this blueprint, I created life on my terms. I became a pro athlete, I was a top salesperson at an international company, I had earned my master's degree... all by 22. It seemed that I had realized all of my dreams by 28. I was a multimillionaire. I was surrounded by friends, splitting my time between New York City and Miami Beach. I was having fun. I was energized, I was constantly inspired and my mind was clear. I was experiencing every bit of success that I had ever envisioned. I was experiencing my Heaven on Earth.

I began to notice that every time life seemed to go off track, there was one common denominator; I had stopped using the blueprint. Every time I utilized it, I expanded and I experienced a life of flow, creating a life of opportunity and freedom. This blueprint was given to me by a superior intelligence than my own brain. I am sharing it as a direct message from the divine and take no credit for inventing it. I am a Messenger, here to guide others in this expansive way of creation.

"I must lead all the beings to nirvana, into that realm of nirvana which leaves nothing behind."
- Buddha

It is my deepest desire to share this blueprint with the world so that all experience Heaven on Earth just as I do. I am grateful to have you on this path. I honor you, I support you and I love you. I am you!

ABOUT EMILY WILSON

At my core, I have always known that everything is in divine order; everything happens for a reason. I held faith that all I desired would find its way to me and that every event and emotion was just another mile on the highway to Heaven.

The moments in my life that I felt most resistance were those where I was out of alignment for the vision I held of what Heaven looked like.

When I worked tirelessly to create something without a clear vision, I ended up in mentally, physically and emotionally abusive situations. Conversely, I found that when I was in alignment with a clear vision, what was once seen as work became play and I experienced flow, grace and ease.

When I allowed opportunity to come to me, I felt my interpretation of success and bliss wash over me. When I fought tooth and nail for any material thing, for a person or for an emotion, I felt depleted and was unappreciative of the outcome, even when it was exactly what I had wanted.

I didn't find joy in what I worked hard for as much as I found joy in what I attracted. I later found out that this is because I am always attracting it that is in vibrational harmony with me.

On my spiritual journey, I discovered that Heaven isn't at the end of the road. Heaven is *everywhere* and Heaven is *now*. With this blueprint, I create Heaven, here, on earth, every moment and I relish in the experience of life exactly a I desire it. My purpose is to share this blueprint with anyone who is experiencing anything other than Heaven on Earth, so that they may live a life full of freedom, empowered to live on their terms and enjoy every moment to the fullest. I am excited to have you on this journey with me and I am already celebrating your success.

Table of Contents

FOREWORD

A few key notes before we begin. Even though this blueprint is co-authored, the majority of the book is in first person singular. This is for several reasons, two of which are:

1. I can only write from my own experience and therefore I can only speak to my own truth.

2. It has been my observation that reading the "I, me & my" has a mysteriously profound impact on the mind of the reader. It seems to paint pictures more vividly and capture the essence of the message in its most pure state.

This blueprint is ever-evolving. I've kept the content to the key elements so that the focus is on the reader's transition to becoming the writer. The reader is to become the one that writes their life into existence on their own terms. Therefore, several examples of each section are available on the resources page online at https://evolvedlife.com/heaven to aid you in writing, expanding upon ideas and guiding you through the process.

In an effort to support the reader in creating their blueprint, I kept the deeper explanations and practices out of this book. Knowing why something works does not make it work any better; for example, knowing how a cell phone works does not give you better service. Instead, I focused on sharing the elements that will transform your life rather than explaining what can be found on the resources page mentioned above.

There may be some terms that are new to you. Feel free to utilize the glossary found at https://evolvedlife.com/glossary which is consistently updated as the English language is constantly expanding.

MY HEAVEN ON EARTH

Creating my Declaration of Heaven on Earth is akin to an architect conceptualizing a building. When a building is erected, the process begins long before materials show up on site. First, the image is conceived in the mind of the architect. Next, he garners the tools necessary to bring this concept from the spiritual plane down to a physical plane. This physical representation of what was once is his mind is called a blueprint. Several versions are created, each adding a new layer of imagination, clarity and detail. This all occurs before construction even begins. The architect envisions what he'd like to create and as he draws this his vision of a completed product he works backwards down to the smallest nuance. He starts with the end in mind. My Heaven on Earth works in a similar fashion.

Many believe Heaven is a place where one goes when the body dies. Life on earth is filled with to-do lists, worry, anxiety and fear. The idea of Heaven on Earth is rarely, if ever, considered a real possibility. I am here to share that Heaven is not only in reach, but already all around. This book is the blueprint for creating Heaven on Earth. Heaven is as I wish to create it. It will be revised time and time again. The practices in this book will bring forth my experience of Heaven on Earth.

I used to think it was because I did something that I created something. I did many things, I saw results, I reached my goals and then I felt great. This model works great until the point when my capacity to do is depleted. It also requires an enormous amount of effort and action, creating stress on the mind and body. This is why so many people stress from burnout, fatigue and disease.

There is also a not-so-obvious problem. For me, the accomplishment of a goal became my motivation the more I accomplished the stronger my ego became. I could not enjoy a single moment unless I was accomplishing. My mind became overdeveloped and my connection to my heart and soul was buried. Finding happiness, love or joy on my exterior accomplishments became elusive and fleeting.

The way I now create is to tap into the divinity within. To embody it that I desire and bring it to me. The required effort is around surrender, rather than my old way, best described as "hard work and hustle." My presence, intention, emotion and attention is all that is required. The life that I desire already exists, it is through the practices outlined in the subsequent pages that I call my experience of reality to me.

My Declaration of My Heaven on Earth

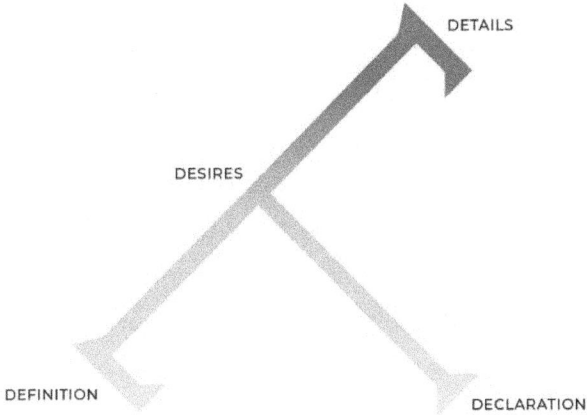

DETAILS

DESIRES

DEFINITION

DECLARATION

Declaration: The formal announcement of the beginning of a state or condition.

My Declaration of Heaven on Earth is the opportunity for me to create the outline of the blueprint which will aid me in bringing my desires to reality. I begin the process by breaking it into five categories: lifestyle, relationships, finances, health and spiritual connection. This allows me to focus on each area independently, to create precision and to expand my imagination in a simple format.

When declaring my desires within each category, I ask myself: *What am I grateful for right now? What areas in my life are causing me discomfort and how would I like to shift them? Where would I like to expand? What areas would I like to bring forth a whole new reality?*

These questions build an outline and give me a starting point. Then, I write down every detail, exactly as I envision it. The more I review My Declaration, detailing the subtleties, the more precision is created. By using numbers, I dive into precision. This also aids me in taking my imagination to deeper depths. Within these depths, opportunities on how to fulfill every detail are revealed to me almost if by magic. It becomes a game I play. The attention alone to thinking and writing about My Declaration often already lifts my mood and I begin to see opportunities.

The first time I used this blueprint it seemed like most everything I wrote down was out of reach. When I shared it with people they laughed. Several years later, I had accomplished or experienced everything I put down on paper. To this day, I am still amazed by how well this formula works. In last year's iteration, I challenged many beliefs I had around physical health. Health appeared to me to be limited by age and was doomed to decline exponentially. Yet, somehow, within only one year, my body remarkably became younger. As I saw what once seemed unbelievable materialize, I found that the only limitation was that of my own imagination. At the time of this writing, it seems that the only limit to creating the reality which I desire is my ability to stretch my imagination, my ability to garner belief and to follow the steps outlined in my blueprint.

I review My Declaration often so that I can make adjustments as my awareness expands. It is one of the highlights of each week. I fall in love with it; the more I fall in love, the faster it comes into my experience.

> *"Anything that the mind can conceive it can achieve."*
> *- Napoleon Hill*

Here is an example of a Declaration by Iain in the Health Category:

My physical body *feels strong, sturdy, powerful, flexible and moves with ease and grace. Physical activities bring me bliss. I learn new skills and movements with ease. I dance to the beat of my own drum and can adapt to any rhythm that comes to my awareness. I love the way I look - muscular, athletic, 6 pack, soft skin with golden radiance. My healthy body inside and out is a foundational component of my identity. My shoulders are broad, posture is perfect, legs are sturdy, chest is defined, my butt is pronounced and toned. My abs are strong and abundant. My erections arrive quickly upon request, are hard and enormous. I have a halo. I can lift or move any fucking thing at any time. My skin is golden and I literally radiate light. I levitate*
My mental body: *I hold my vision in my thoughts at all times. I realize the opportunities in every situation, stay centered and leverage those opportunities to their greatest. I detach quickly from thoughts of less empowering paradigms and easily integrate expanded empowering paradigms. I hold attention to that which I intend to create. I am intentional with all of my thoughts. I channel my heart's intentions. My memory is photographic. I easily decipher what happened and use it to leverage my empowering beliefs. My thoughts keep me steered*

towards manifesting my heaven on earth. I am telepathic. I am in tune. I "think: less which conserves energy for my energetic body.

My energetic body: *I sleep an average of 4-7 hours a day and feel full of grounded powerful energy during my waking hours. I channel divine energy through me which keeps me in a state of peak performance. Short periods of rest allow me to integrate and embody expanded states. My energetic body raises the vibe of everything that comes within my field of awareness.*

My emotional body: *My default emotion is of divine love. Emotions move through me quickly and I use the energy provided by each emotion to embody and radiate all that I choose to create each day. I project divine love infinitely from my heart which raises the vibe all those who come into my awareness to a state of joy, love, play, bliss. I experience orgasmic, climax simply by holding it in my heart intention. The power of emotion aids in attracting my expanding versions of Heaven on Earth at all times.*

My mind, emotions, physical body and spirit are aligned. All this and better!

The Adventure of My Heaven on Earth

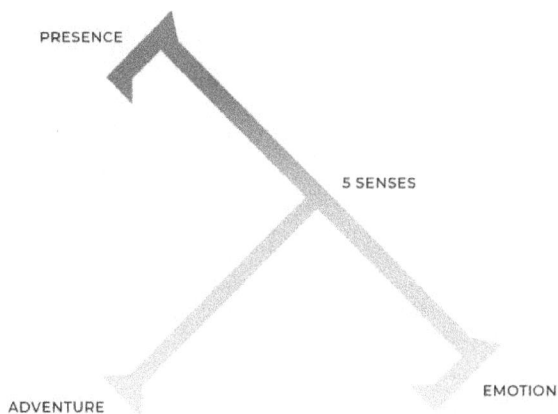

Adventure: Daring and exciting activity calling for enterprise and enthusiasm.

Once I have written my current Declaration of each category, I create the Adventure. This is a really exciting part, as I am writing the storyline of how I will experience the unfolding of My Declaration. I do this by creating a detailed description of what and how I'd like to experience life. Here, I immerse myself in the emotion of how it feels to embody what I have created. I close my eyes and I live it, tapping into the smell, the sight, the sound, the taste and the feeling of all that I desire.` I am experiencing Heaven on Earth on the mental plane in a heightened state, which supercharges its manifestation. My capacity to believe in what was once out of reach increases and the power of faith supports me in creating my manifestation.

I embark on the journey of living this reality, narrating a storyline that stimulates all five senses. By leveraging the power of emotions, I build the bridge between the spiritual and the physical. When I am worried or in fear, I will create more of the same. The same is true when I hold joy, love and gratitude in my awareness. This took some practice for me at first. With patience and tenacity it became second nature. By embracing a clear sensory description throughout the story of The Adventure here on earth, I intentionally begin to manifest it. Here, I leverage the power of creation, the laws of vibration and the laws of attraction to bring what I desire most to me.

Once I have the clear description of The Adventure, I fill it with descriptive, stimulating words so that I am taken into the experience. The more nuanced and subtle, the better. It may at first feel awkward and uncomfortable; it may flow with ease. This practice will expand the energy that is put into it. Each draft expands into further drafts over time and will never actually be complete, as I plan to forever write my life into existence. If at any point I no longer enjoy reading The Adventure, or would like to change course, I start by revisiting the entire section. So long as I read it often I rarely have to make large changes; like a jet flying cross country, there are constant minor adjustments to course-correct - maximizing impact and minimizing effort.

I review The Adventure sections often which both creates new and strengthens existing empowering neuro-pathways in my mind. Reviewing brings it into my conscious awareness and the repetition makes it so the subconscious is actively working on all that has been written even when my conscious attention is elsewhere.

Here is an example of Iain's Adventure in Relationships:

My Self:

As I open my eyes each day I feel a blessing to be alive. My body is full of energy ready for anything. I feel grounded with a solid foundation that allows me to reach out infinitely. I am calm and collected with infinite power ready to be exercised at any moment. I am present to the now and can feel the divine loving lifeforce that I am flow through me. Each cell is filled with golden light. My chakras are ignited and spin in harmony. My mind is still and ready to fulfill the desires of my heart & soul. I feel the strength and power of each cell of my body. I feel the flexibility and agility of soft tissues in my body. I can smell the earth that my body is created from. I can hear the hum of my energetic body vibrating in harmony with nature. I embody and radiate divine love from all that I am. When I look inward I see golden light and feel warmth radiating from my core.

My One:

When I am with my partner I feel an energetic connection that bonds us uniquely together. I feel my heart and loins pull towards her and hers towards mine. She gives herself to me fully and I receive her energy. I give myself to her fully and she receives me. Our way of being together is as important and seamless as inhalation and exhalation.

She walks into the room and I feel the warmth and radiance of her energy well before she is in sight. My hair on the back of my neck rises up, heart beats slightly faster and is filled with warmth. The charge runs down my spine igniting each of my chakras and blood immediately flows to my dick. She attempts to sneak up behind me quietly running my direction. I hear her squeal as she explodes lovingly leaping in my direction. I turn in the knick of time and she falls into my arms, or jumps on me to straddle my torso and she kisses me. Her supple lips soften against mine. The taste within her mouth is sweet and distinctly of her. Her scent of life, youth, joy is like a bouquet of the finest flowers. We laugh together with gratitude and amazement that we have found each other. The way her skin feels against mine stimulates my body with electricity. I feel wholeness within, a new level of completion and presence as I can see the world through her eyes and my own simultaneously. I fall into an infinite abyss of love. The line of where I end and where she begins seems to dissolve. I feel a sense of power and confidence exploding throughout my body. I gaze into her eyes and know in each moment I am exactly where I belong to be.

My Family & Friends:

My family and friends come together to celebrate and honor my contributions. They are always giving me gifts. Toasts with mocktails and juices are made in celebration of the great health and love that they are experiencing as a result of Evolved Life and using the Heaven on Earth Manifesto. I hear the sounds of laughter as days of past are remembered with comedy, joy and love. I hear excitement and inspiration in voices as we talk about the now and the soon to be now, which at one point was called the future. We all come together and merge our vision of heaven on earth - which allows us to build the new kingdom together. Together we hold on to our vision and bring it to us.

Mind, emotion and soul are in perfect vibration. The room is silent, yet I can hear a hum. All are still yet, movement is prevalent. We see everything, yet our eyes are closed. We are united in truth and love.

Heaven on Earth is here, and so it is...

LIFE CATEGORIES

The five life categories I choose to focus on are outlined below. More categories could be added however I found this extra work to be less impactful than sticking to these key areas. At one point, I had 13 different categories. My Heaven on Earth blueprint was over 200 pages. It became too much to keep up with and pushed me off of my path. These 5 key areas have consistently kept me on course and done so with ease. Feel free to add more categories or remove categories as you see fit; after all, this is your Heaven on Earth.

Important: I create a draft copy or bulleted outline of each category before moving to the next and suggest the reader does the same. The moment I put pen to paper manifestation has occurred and my mind will begin to expand in the background. The first word is the hardest so start writing something even if only one word before moving on to the next. Reading this book in its entirety without participating will yield few results. Following the blueprint as outlined will yield Heaven on Earth.

Health

"A Healthy Person has 1,000 wishes and a Sick person has 1 wish."
- *Indian Proverb*

I find my health to be one of the most important. Without great health, it is very challenging to experience greatness in other areas of life. It also seems to be one of the most tangible. I break down it down into subsections. In these sections, I describe how I optimize and relate to each one of my bodies. When each of these four bodies are in harmony, magic occurs.

My Physical Body largely encompasses how my body actually looks and feels. I also include how it feels to be inside of my body and the way I experience the movement of it.

My Energetic Body is composed of how my energy is distributed throughout the day and how I utilize rest to recharge.

My Mental Body determines which thoughts are brought into my awareness so that I experience life on terms. This allows me to maintain thoughts that are in alignment with my soul's purpose.

My Emotional Body defines how and which emotions I intend to use to create my manifestations in the physical world. I also use this as a place to alchemize or transmute any emotions that I experience which may be of a lower vibration than my natural state; at my current level of awareness, my natural state is 'divine love.' This is a deep sense of unconditional love without attachment; it's depths are infinite and I am only at the precipice of grasping the words to describe it.

MY DECLARATION

MY ADVENTURE

Relationships

Relationship: The way in which two or more people are connected, or the state of being connected.

The relationships portion of *My Heaven on Earth* exists to allow me to create relationship scenarios so that I can connect intentionally with all the people I meet. It gives me purpose, clarity and enhances my experience in all of my relationships. These are broken into sections. This allows me to set intentions to relate to people under different circumstances.

My Self is the relationship I have with myself, answering who I believe I am and my default state of being.

My One is my intimate partnership, the person who is secondary to my primary relationship with myself. My closest chosen mirror.

My Friends and Family is where I set the intention for the relationships with those closest to me. When I have children I may break this out into a separate section; it is up to the reader to make this choice.

My Work Relationships is where I design how I interact with others when connecting business matters.

MY DECLARATION

MY ADVENTURE

Spiritual Connection

In the spiritual connection section, I define how I connect with a higher power of guidance: the divine. For some, the divine may be God, imagination, source, the universe or energy. I include all in my definition of a higher power. I like to key in by referring to this energy as *the force of life that runs through me*. It is my innerstanding that life is designed to perpetuate itself, to expand into the infinite expression of existence. By connecting to this power, it is clear that I can create anything by tapping into it and bringing it through me. With this in mind, I am more than my thoughts, body, emotions, job title or anything that I may have once identified with on this physical plane. I become the observer and can create from a higher level of awareness. By connecting to this force of life and expanding my ability to radiate it, I can project anything, as it all already exists, into my surroundings.

It is important to foster this connection in whichever way I am called to. This could mean attending church, praying, meditating, practicing yoga, gardening, playing a sport, discovering a new hobby or activity. It could be all of these ways. This is a practice that aids me in becoming very present to the moment, which is where I can be open to intuition or guidance. It may even give me great clarity. I may even become one with this energy discarding the attachment to the physical plane. My relationship and how I connect is entirely up to my choosing.

MY DECLARATION

_____

_____

_____

_____

_____

_____

_____

_____

_____

_____

_____

_____

_____

MY ADVENTURE

_____

_____

_____

_____

_____

_____

_____

_____

_____

_____

_____

_____

_____

_____

Finances

In relation to finances, I investigate how I relate to and experience money. This includes both how I earn and how I manage my money. My beliefs around money are clearly defined. The purpose behind how I use money is clear so that I use money and it does not use me.

When I held the belief that money was the root of all evil, I would push it or anyone with it away subconsciously. I may shun it or even use it for evil myself. When I believe that money is a tool or an energetic currency in which I receive as I give, then money flows into my life as I say so and as I see deserving. This is just one example of a plethora of beliefs around money. At the time of this writing, I view money as a tool that allows me to positively impact the life of myself and others. It flows like a river, which is why the term liquidity is used in relation to money.

MY DECLARATION

_____

_____

_____

_____

_____

_____

_____

_____

_____

_____

_____

_____

_____

MY ADVENTURE

_____

_____

_____

_____

_____

_____

_____

_____

_____

_____

_____

_____

_____

_____

Lifestyle

Lifestyle: The way in which a person or group lives.

The lifestyle vision is used to intentionally attract the desired experience of my way of life. For example, when traveling, some people prefer the opulence of 5 star resorts while others prefer to go camping and pitch a tent. Some may choose to go Glamping, a combination of the two where they are embedded in the forest and still have the luxuries they desire. Some people don't even travel. No matter what my preferred way of life is, creating a Declaration and mapping out the Adventure are critical elements in bringing it forth. Lifestyle includes my experiences, surroundings and material items.

Questions to ask myself:

Where am I?
Who and what am I surrounded by?
What recreational activities do I participate in?
Where is my time directed?
Do I drive a SUV, sports car, sedan or even have a driver?
What does my home look like?
How often do I travel?

MY DECLARATION

MY ADVENTURE

MY RITUAL EXPLAINED

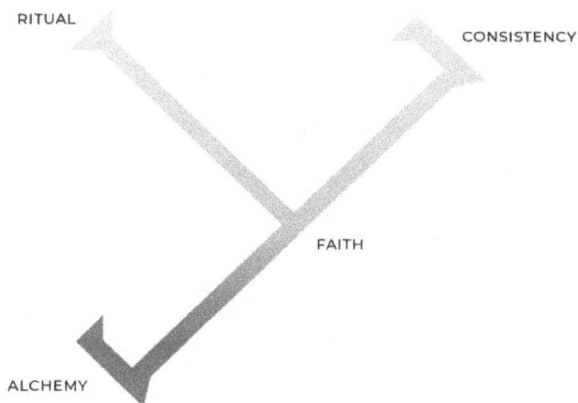

RITUAL

CONSISTENCY

FAITH

ALCHEMY

Ritual: A series of actions or a type of behavior regularly and invariably followed by someone.

The Ritual is the "compass" of making my Heaven on Earth a reality. When designing my daily practice, I keep my intended creation of Heaven on Earth at the forefront of my mind. In the spiritual realm, this ensures that my thoughts are in alignment with My Declaration. On the physical plane, this reminds me to be sure that the words and actions I take over the course of the day are in alignment with My Declaration. This ritual keeps my emotions in the highest vibration and ensures that each day unfolds bringing me closer to or experiencing Heaven on Earth.

This can become really fun. I like to think of it as if I am playing the role of a Casting Director, casting myself as my desired role each day. I get to choose who I will be and how to leverage that state of being to make sure each day is one of my own creation and is in alignment. This is literally my compass to make sure I am experiencing my Heaven on Earth each day.

Through repetition of practicing this ritual daily, the mind creates and strengthens new neural pathways consciously, creating my chosen manifestation. I also find that the daily practice is inspiring, as I often see how my declaration of Heaven on Earth is quickly becoming my reality. There are countless additional benefits to the daily practice which are best left to be revealed throughout the process.

In the following pages you will find the ritual. Use this book as your journal and write in these pages daily. There is something about writing versus typing that causes manifestation to occur faster. Some say it is because it takes more effort, while others suggest it is because of the emotion that is experienced as pen hits paper. For most people, there is more dopamine released when writing than when typing. It has been proven that writing aids in sharpening memory recall and improving critical thinking. There are about 40 hand movements made while typing and over 14,000 by writing. This is a clear signal to the brain that what I am writing is important. Whatever the case, I invite you to write in this book each day and follow the format of this ritual. You will find that Heaven has always been in your reach and is already here in the the now, waiting for you to clearly request it to come in to physical form for you." this paragraph was added to the last page of the document in the "Final Thoughts" chapter.

TITLE _In the Now, I Create_

DAY _1 : 1_

My current state is...

- _Emotionally, I am clear, happy, fresh._
- _Energetically, exhausted, feeling weighed down physically_
- _because of my migraine. Also feeling a little weak in_
- _the muscles. Mentally, I am a little clouded. My_
- _thoughts do not feel directed. Spiritually, I am divine._

Today, I choose to hold myself to my highest and greatest, pointed in the direction of my vision of Heaven on Earth.

I upgrade my current state to...

- _Emotionally, in the new! Feeling pure bliss in every_
- _moment. Energetically on fire, propelled through my_
- _day with ease. Physically, strong. My body supports_
- _me in the ways I desire. Mentally, sharp, focused_
- _and productive. Spiritually, I am divine and I_
- _create all that is divine around me._

Today, I am... _Focused Freedom_

The following core values and emotions will support my greatness.	_love_	_presence_	_focus_	_surrender_

I choose to immediately adopt the following belief upgrades:

Belief	Upgraded Belief
There is not enough time to get everything done.	Everything is in divine order and is already complete.
My headache will keep me from completing my work.	My body fuels me as I request

As my day flows in harmony, I will...

- ☐ do my Divine Tide
- ☐ read
- ☐ client meeting @ 2 PM
- ☐ create (music, writing, drawing, whatever calls)
- ☐ finalize book & send to designer

My gifts that will aid in the fulfilment of these goals are...

my creativity, my ability to surrender
and fall into the moment, my authenticity,
my boldness, my unconditional self love.

NOTES:

Title

With the Title, I give a name to the landscape on which my character plays. I title my day as I would title a movie, a chapter in a book, a poem or a song, describing the overarching theme or action of what is to unfold. It may be abstract and coy or straightforward and bold.

On a day where I am looking to experience divine love, my title may be "Discovering Divine Love."

On a day where I am locking down investors for a new project, my title may be "Manifesting Millions Like a Boss."

Day

This can be the calendar date. This can be a marker for how many days I have been on the journey of creating my Heaven on Earth. This can be an infinity sign, as time is a mere illusion created by the mind. This can be a number signifying a verse, like in a holy scripture, as I am literally writing my version of the bible as I experience it. I choose to mark my days in the case that I return to it for future reflection or to see how far I've come.

My Current State

Here, I assess my state in the present moment. I explore every atom of my physical being, spiritual connection, mental realm of thoughts, emotions and energetic body to bring both the light and the pollution to the surface. I really dive into it. When I choose to ignore my pain points, I will remain in pain. When I choose to hide my greatness, it will remain unseen. By assessing the truth about where I am, I am priming myself to release and transform it. Transformation is done in my desired state next.

Icons:

♨	My Emotional Body (emotions)
✿	My Energetic Body (energy level and coherence)
𝍃	My Physical Body (ail physical feelings)
♀	My Mental Body (thoughts)
◈	My Soul (connection to higher power or life force)

Questions to ask myself:

What thoughts and emotions are passing through me in this moment? Are they in alignment with my Declaration and Adventure?

Am I connected to my spirit? Is my intuition flowing through?

How is my physical body feeling? Are there any aches and pains to be aware of? Am I feeling healthy or sick in anyway?

Where is my energy level? Am I attached to any external energies? These external energies may come from work, relationships or even hot current events. Do I feel calm and centered or is my energy unfocused and frazzled?

My Desired State

By writing my intended state of being, I actually begin to transmute my current state into my desired state.

This step is extremely effective. Why? Because the mind is so efficient that thoughts will loop until I consciously redirect them. Here I am redirecting my mental energy. When I am thinking about a scenario, my mind will delve deeper into that thought when left unattended. Those thoughts will then release hormones which causes me to experience certain emotions. Those emotions will then bring about words and actions that are in kind. When I write out my desired state of being, I break that loop and immediately begin to redirect my state of being to aiding in the creation I've outlined for myself. At times, I may only be aware of the emotion I am experiencing. In this case, I can remember what I was thinking about before the emotion to reveal its source. This is actually a fun practice, yet unnecessary. This ritual will begin transform my emotions, as soon as, I write down my Desired State.

When I am upset, I will act and speak as an upset person; this, in turn, creates more situations that will upset me. When I am in love, I will act and speak as a loving person; this, in turn, brings about more experiences of love. When this is applied, scenarios that previously would have resulted in disaster begin to reveal opportunities. Synchronistic surprises often seem to come about as well.

There was one distinction that helped me to understand why this is so effective. Emotions and thoughts are not me, they are simply visitors. By having awareness around my thoughts, I can redirect them down a new path. Having awareness around emotions that are in my field allows me to redirect my current e-motion (energy in motion.) I can then use this energy to bring about My Declaration as described in The Adventure.

To accomplish this I review my answers to my current state and then rewrite the states to match the state in which I desire. My only limit is my own ability to believe or imagine. In only a few moments, what may have started as the worst of days can be transformed.

It is important to note that I speak and write these answers in the present tense, in order to initiate the embodiment of this desired state of being.

I Am

Here, I really dive deeply into the role of Casting Director. I define my role or persona for the day. Who I choose to be on any given day will yield results of kind, so choosing the "who" that aids me in bringing my Declaration and the Adventure to life is paramount.

On a Sunday with my family, I may choose to be the best spouse, parent, sibling or friend ever.

On a Monday at work I may choose to be the most impactful, heart centered entrepreneur who ever lived.

I may even choose to be someone abstract like The Observer. I can also choose to embody an emotion. This may be divine love, in which case I would state "I am Divine Love." Other examples may include Compassion, Kindness, Optimism and Pure Joy.

By choosing to embody a specific emotion, I can be sure to project my energy onto all that comes into my awareness and eventually experience that emotion reflecting back onto me.

My Greatness

In order for anything to be great, there must be a solid foundation and structural integrity. For this section, I elect four core values or emotions that will aid me in expressing my greatness and supporting the role that I have chosen for myself for the day.

My favorites are Love, Freedom, Power and Wholeness. These change when presented with different circumstances in my life. I may call on courage when I am challenged. I may call on compassion when surrounded by people who appear to be less fortunate.
Some examples include:

Honesty, Integrity, Compassion, Loyalty, Responsiveness, Precision, Faith, Courage, Strength and so on.

My Beliefs

The mind creates reality based on what it believes to be true. It is incredibly persistent, which is why changing habits can be a considerable challenge for many. Rather than using willpower to change a habit, I return to the core and discover what I fundamentally believe to be true about the current situation; I determine if that belief is empowering me to live my Declaration and Adventure.

Some popular beliefs that are disempowering in the western culture are:

- I am not lovable.
- I don't have enough time.
- I'm bad at communicating.
- I am not pretty/handsome.
- It requires hard work to make money.
- I am not appreciated.

When I believe these to be true, every word, gesture, action and occurrence that comes into my awareness will be seen through this lens. I will give meaning to everything I experience, framed by this disempowering belief.

The solution is to identify these existing beliefs, to create empowering beliefs and to practice them vigilantly.

There are dozens of effective ways to make this change. Here, I share what I find to be one of the most simplistic ways to transform beliefs. Other resources to dive deeper into belief hacking can be found at evolvedlife.com/heaven

Step 1 I list out any disempowering beliefs that may have popped into my mind during my present state.
Step 2 Rewrite them into the chosen empowering belief. This can usually by removing the word "not" or by changing a "disempowering" word into an "empowering" word.
Step 3 Read each empowering belief at minimum 3x a day until it is embodied.

Step 4 Always be available to upgrading every belief so that my Declaration can eternally be expanding.

My Intentions

Now comes the time to create a list of intentions that I am feeling inspired to or am being guided to partake in for the day. This is not a to-do list. This is a list of intended outcomes. At the end of the day I will have...

I may "make" them happen by doing, I may "watch" them happen by synchronistic alignment or I may delegate them to someone else.

No matter what has been accomplished at the end of the day, I know that all outcomes are exactly what they are supposed to be. By maintaining this attitude, I experience great flow and more of my desired results occur. I also leave room for even better results to come to fruition. All that energy I used to use for control becomes a force for attraction and creation.

My Gifts

Remembering how gifted I already am is a great way to see how I can aid in bringing My Declaration and The Adventure to life. These gifts can be anything from a skill that I've developed to a talent that comes naturally. They may even present themselves as a way of being.

So, which of my gifts will I exercise today as I take action in the fulfillment of the goals that I have set?

I have listed some examples of each of these types of gifts.

Vocabulary	Speed	Bravery	Tenacity
Will Power	Writing Skills	Charm	Dancing
Knowledge of...	Ability to...	Curiosity	Stamina
Detail	Playfulness	Compassion	Sales

Notes:

I use this area for a variety of different items. Most common are:

- Logging any mysterious coincidences, synchronicities, that show up and aid in my experience of Heaven on Earth which I usually refer to as diving alignment.

- Tracking distinctions and insights. Like the moment I realized that I was the observer of my thoughts and became disassociated with them.

- Ideas that I may choose to add to My Declaration or The Adventure

- Ideas I'd like to share with someone important to me.

Expansion

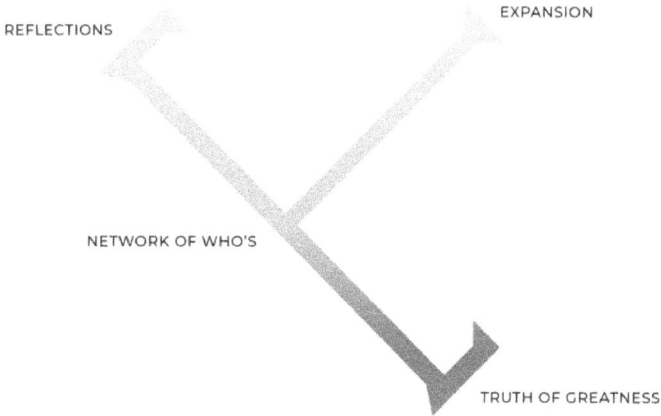

REFLECTIONS

EXPANSION

NETWORK OF WHO'S

TRUTH OF GREATNESS

"You are the average of the five people you spend the most time with."
- Jim Rohn

By creating a Declaration, the Adventure and practicing a powerful ritual, I have consistently been able create my Heaven on Earth. However, the element that can truly accelerate success is surrounding myself with the right people. Having a community of individuals who offer support, guidance and expansion is paramount to creating Heaven on Earth. Here are some quick strategies on how I make sure that the people who are around me are going to aid me along my quest.

To begin, I invite friends and family over to share the contents of this book especially My Declarations and The Adventure portions that I have written. This immediately will get their minds to work on my behalf. If I say I'd like to learn how to draw each person who hears this will think about who they know that could teach me, or other ways I might learn. Everyone who knows my vision of Heaven on Earth will come to support me.

This will also weed out those who do not support me and shows me who in my field is actually interested in improving their life. It tells me who is ready to speak the same language and live a life pointed towards creating their Heaven on Earth. When I invited them over for a party, they would come; when I invited them for dinner, they were there; when I invited them to go watch "the game," they were all about it. Now that it is time to create the reality of my dreams, are they with me?

In my case, it was only a small fraction that were truly interested in creating the life they claimed they wanted. Very few were up for the challenge. The very mysterious and interesting outcome was that those who were interested showed up 100%; some of them even invited others and all of a sudden my group had expanded. Then, after a few of my friends started seeing the amazing results, the old friends who were initially resistant wanted in.

I share my Declaration with as many people as possible. As mentioned earlier, this is literally speaking it into existence. The other benefit is that this will elicit a response from whomever I am sharing with. It becomes quite clear if they are going to support me or hold me back.

Those that are holding me back are going to tell me all of the reasons why what I have declared will not work or why it is unrealistic. I find these individuals to be distracting; for them, every solution has a problem. For a long time, I kept these people in my life out of loyalty or out of a desire to bring them with me. It would feel like I was swimming upstream and often I'd find myself regressing into my old ways, off of my new path.

Those that are going to aid me in my quest will be eager to help me expand My Declaration, helping me to see opportunities that I may have missed, introducing me to other people that are creating or have already created similar things, and so on. These individuals may be in the vast minority. At first for me, it was so rare to find one that I almost gave up several times. It was when I started to say "no" to all those who were not supporting me that I finally made room for the high-vibrational individuals to show up.

Building a community can be time consuming and expensive. Over 5 years, I spent over a quarter of a million dollars traveling to find these individuals and bring them into the Evolved Life community, some into the group programs and others into the Facebook group. Joining both of these groups is the fastest way to expand one's network to a group of curated individuals that speak the same language. There are many other ways to do this, however this is the most simplistic and seems to be the most effective.

FINAL THOUGHTS

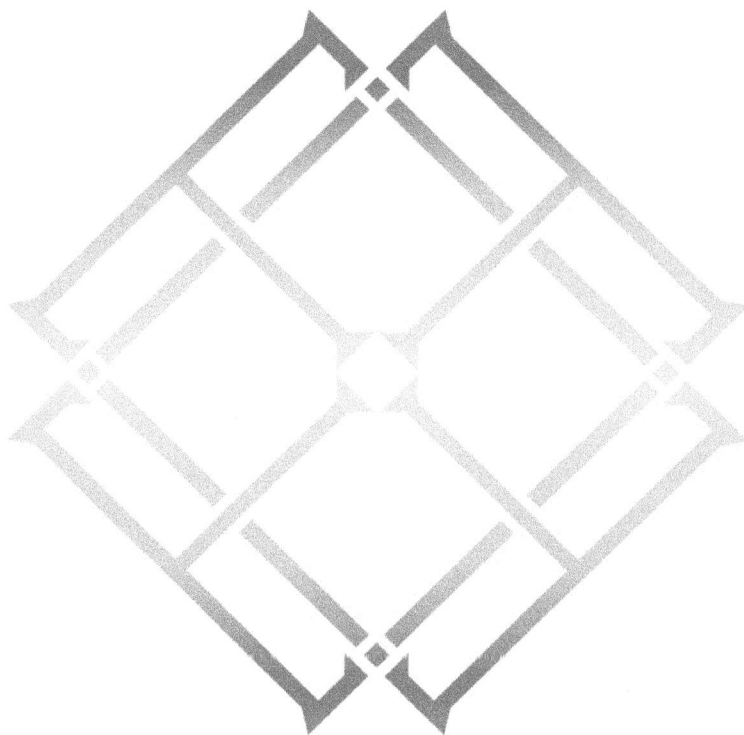

You now have the blueprint that I have used to create my Heaven on Earth. I use these practices so that I can continue to expand what heaven means to me. I find that that more that I practice, the better the world seems to become. In my current reality I am surrounded by the deepest depths of love, my health is extraordinary, my finances are solid, my connection to the divine life force that flows through me expands infinitely and my lifestyle is exactly where I envisioned it being in the blueprint I had created a year ago. Yet I am still expanding.

Now, my purpose is to aid others in this amazing experience. Now that I am experiencing it for myself, I am envisioning a world of peace, opulence, abundance and love. I trust that you will make great use of this material so that when our paths cross I can hear how you've ushered in your Heaven on Earth and how you are positively impacting the lives of those around you while doing so.

TITLE _____

DAY   _____

My current state is...

🔥 ....
⚛ ....
𐀀 ....
💭 ....
◈ ....

Today, I choose to hold myself to my highest and greatest, pointed in the direction of my vision of heaven on Earth.

I upgrade my current state to...

🔥 ....
⚛ ....
𐀀 ....
💭 ....
◈ ....

Today, I am...

The following core
values and emotions
will support my
greatness

I choose to immediately adopt the following belief upgrades:

Belief	Upgraded Belief

As my day flows in harmony, I will...

☐
☐
☐
☐
☐

My gifts that will aid in the fulfilment of those goals are...

NOTES:

TITLE _____

DAY   _____

My current state is...

◉ ....
✿ ....
大 ....
○ ....
◈ ....

Today, I choose to hold myself to my highest and greatest, pointed in the direction of my vision of heaven on Earth.

I upgrade my current state to...

◉ ....
✿ ....
大 ....
○ ....
◈ ....

Today, I am...

The following core
values and emotions
will support my
greatness

I choose to immediately adopt the following belief upgrades:

Belief	Upgraded Belief

As my day flows in harmony, I will...

- ☐
- ☐
- ☐
- ☐
- ☐

My gifts that will aid in the fulfilment of those goals are...

_____

_____

_____

NOTES:

TITLE _____

DAY   _____

My current state is…

🜂 _____
❀ _____
🧍 _____
💭 _____
◈ _____

Today, I choose to hold myself to my highest and greatest, pointed in the direction of my vision of heaven on Earth.

I upgrade my current state to…

🜂 _____
❀ _____
🧍 _____
💭 _____
◈ _____

Today, I am...

The following core
values and emotions
will support my
greatness

I choose to immediately adopt the following belief upgrades:

Belief	Upgraded Belief

As my day flows in harmony, I will...

- ☐
- ☐
- ☐
- ☐
- ☐

My gifts that will aid in the fulfilment of those goals are...

_____

_____

_____

NOTES:

TITLE   _____

DAY   _____

My current state is...

    🔥 _____

    ✿ _____

    🖈 _____

    💬 _____

    ◈ _____

Today, I choose to hold myself to my highest and greatest, pointed in the direction of my vision of heaven on Earth.

I upgrade my current state to...

    🔥 _____

    ✿ _____

    🖈 _____

    💬 _____

    ◈ _____

Today, I am...

The following core
values and emotions
will support my
greatness

I choose to immediately adopt the following belief upgrades:

Belief	Upgraded Belief

As my day flows in harmony, I will...

- ☐
- ☐
- ☐
- ☐
- ☐

My gifts that will aid in the fulfilment of those goals are...

_____

_____

_____

NOTES:

TITLE _____

DAY   _____

My current state is...

◌ ....
✿ ....
𐀪 ....
◌ ....
◈ ....

Today, I choose to hold myself to my highest and greatest, pointed in the direction of my vision of heaven on Earth.

I upgrade my current state to...

◌ ....
✿ ....
𐀪 ....
◌ ....
◈ ....

Today, I am...

The following core
values and emotions
will support my
greatness

I choose to immediately adopt the following belief upgrades:

Belief	Upgraded Belief

As my day flows in harmony, I will...

☐

☐

☐

☐

☐

My gifts that will aid in the fulfilment of those goals are...

NOTES:

TITLE _____

DAY _____

My current state is...

    🔥 _____
    ⚛ _____
    🧍 _____
    💭 _____
    ◈ _____

Today, I choose to hold myself to my highest and greatest, pointed in the direction of my vision of heaven on Earth.

I upgrade my current state to...

    🔥 _____
    ⚛ _____
    🧍 _____
    💭 _____
    ◈ _____

Today, I am...

The following core
values and emotions
will support my
greatness

I choose to immediately adopt the following belief upgrades:

Belief	Upgraded Belief

As my day flows in harmony, I will...

- ☐
- ☐
- ☐
- ☐
- ☐

My gifts that will aid in the fulfilment of those goals are...

NOTES:

TITLE _____

DAY   _____

My current state is...

◉ ....
❀ ....
🕴 ....
💬 ....
◈ ....

Today, I choose to hold myself to my highest and greatest, pointed in the direction of my vision of heaven on Earth.

I upgrade my current state to...

◉ ....
❀ ....
🕴 ....
💬 ....
◈ ....

Today, I am...

The following core
values and emotions
will support my
greatness

I choose to immediately adopt the following belief upgrades:

Belief	Upgraded Belief

As my day flows in harmony, I will...

- ☐
- ☐
- ☐
- ☐
- ☐

My gifts that will aid in the fulfilment of those goals are...

NOTES:

TITLE _____

DAY   _____

My current state is…

◊ _____

❀ _____

✝ _____

○ _____

◈ _____

Today, I choose to hold myself to my highest and greatest, pointed in the direction of my vision of heaven on Earth.

I upgrade my current state to…

◊ _____

❀ _____

✝ _____

○ _____

◈ _____

Today, I am…

The following core values and emotions will support my greatness

I choose to immediately adopt the following belief upgrades:

Belief	Upgraded Belief

As my day flows in harmony, I will...

☐
☐
☐
☐
☐

My gifts that will aid in the fulfilment of those goals are...

NOTES:

TITLE _____

DAY   _____

My current state is...

� _____
❀ _____
🕇 _____
◯ _____
◈ _____

Today, I choose to hold myself to my highest and greatest, pointed in the direction of my vision of heaven on Earth.

I upgrade my current state to...

◉ _____
❀ _____
🕇 _____
◯ _____
◈ _____

Today, I am...

The following core values and emotions will support my greatness			

I choose to immediately adopt the following belief upgrades:

Belief	Upgraded Belief

As my day flows in harmony, I will...

☐
☐
☐
☐
☐

My gifts that will aid in the fulfilment of those goals are...

_____

_____

_____

NOTES:

TITLE _____

DAY _____

My current state is...

🔥 ....
❀ ....
🕴 ....
💭 ....
◈ ....

Today, I choose to hold myself to my highest and greatest, pointed in the direction of my vision of heaven on Earth.

I upgrade my current state to...

🔥 ....
❀ ....
🕴 ....
💭 ....
◈ ....

Today, I am...

The following core
values and emotions
will support my
greatness

I choose to immediately adopt the following belief upgrades:

Belief	Upgraded Belief

As my day flows in harmony, I will...

- ☐
- ☐
- ☐
- ☐
- ☐

My gifts that will aid in the fulfilment of those goals are...

NOTES:

TITLE _____

DAY   _____

My current state is…

- _____
- _____
- _____
- _____
- _____

Today, I choose to hold myself to my highest and greatest, pointed in the direction of my vision of heaven on Earth.

I upgrade my current state to…

- _____
- _____
- _____
- _____
- _____

Today, I am...

The following core
values and emotions
will support my
greatness

I choose to immediately adopt the following belief upgrades:

Belief	Upgraded Belief

As my day flows in harmony, I will...

☐

☐

☐

☐

☐

My gifts that will aid in the fulfilment of those goals are...

NOTES:

TITLE _____

DAY _____

My current state is…

🔥 _____
✿ _____
🧍 _____
💬 _____
◈ _____

Today, I choose to hold myself to my highest and greatest, pointed in the direction of my vision of heaven on Earth.

I upgrade my current state to…

🔥 _____
✿ _____
🧍 _____
💬 _____
◈ _____

Today, I am...

The following core
values and emotions
will support my
greatness

I choose to immediately adopt the following belief upgrades:

Belief	Upgraded Belief

As my day flows in harmony, I will…

☐
☐
☐
☐
☐

My gifts that will aid in the fulfilment of those goals are…

NOTES:

TITLE _____

DAY   _____

My current state is…

🔥 ....
⚛ ....
🯅 ....
💭 ....
◈ ....

Today, I choose to hold myself to my highest and greatest, pointed in the direction of my vision of heaven on Earth.

I upgrade my current state to…

🔥 ....
⚛ ....
🯅 ....
💭 ....
◈ ....

Today, I am...

The following core
values and emotions
will support my
greatness

I choose to immediately adopt the following belief upgrades:

Belief	Upgraded Belief

As my day flows in harmony, I will...

- ☐
- ☐
- ☐
- ☐
- ☐

My gifts that will aid in the fulfilment of those goals are...

NOTES:

TITLE _____

DAY   _____

My current state is…

🔥 ···

❀ ···

𝄉 ···

☁ ···

◈ ···

Today, I choose to hold myself to my highest and greatest,
pointed in the direction of my vision of heaven on Earth.

I upgrade my current state to…

🔥 ···

❀ ···

𝄉 ···

☁ ···

◈ ···

Today, I am...

The following core
values and emotions
will support my
greatness

I choose to immediately adopt the following belief upgrades:

Belief	Upgraded Belief

As my day flows in harmony, I will...

☐
☐
☐
☐
☐

My gifts that will aid in the fulfilment of those goals are...

NOTES:

TITLE _____

DAY   _____

My current state is...

◔ ....
❀ ....
⫟ ....
◔ ....
◈ ....

Today, I choose to hold myself to my highest and greatest, pointed in the direction of my vision of heaven on Earth.

I upgrade my current state to...

◔ ....
❀ ....
⫟ ....
◔ ....
◈ ....

Today, I am...

The following core
values and emotions
will support my
greatness

I choose to immediately adopt the following belief upgrades:

Belief	Upgraded Belief

As my day flows in harmony, I will...

- ☐
- ☐
- ☐
- ☐
- ☐

My gifts that will aid in the fulfilment of those goals are...

_____

_____

_____

NOTES:

TITLE _____

DAY   _____

My current state is...

- 🔥 ....
- ✿ ....
- 🧍 ....
- 💭 ....
- ◈ ....

Today, I choose to hold myself to my highest and greatest, pointed in the direction of my vision of heaven on Earth.

I upgrade my current state to...

- 🔥 ....
- ✿ ....
- 🧍 ....
- 💭 ....
- ◈ ....

Today, I am...

The following core
values and emotions
will support my
greatness

I choose to immediately adopt the following belief upgrades:

Belief	Upgraded Belief

As my day flows in harmony, I will...

- ☐
- ☐
- ☐
- ☐
- ☐

My gifts that will aid in the fulfilment of those goals are...

NOTES:

TITLE _____

DAY _____

My current state is…

�
  🔥 _____
  ❀ _____
  🕇 _____
  💭 _____
  ◈ _____

Today, I choose to hold myself to my highest and greatest, pointed in the direction of my vision of heaven on Earth.

I upgrade my current state to…

  🔥 _____
  ❀ _____
  🕇 _____
  💭 _____
  ◈ _____

Today, I am...

The following core
values and emotions
will support my
greatness

I choose to immediately adopt the following belief upgrades:

Belief	Upgraded Belief

As my day flows in harmony, I will...

- ☐
- ☐
- ☐
- ☐
- ☐

My gifts that will aid in the fulfilment of those goals are...

NOTES:

TITLE _____

DAY _____

My current state is...

   🔥 _____
   ⚛ _____
   🧍 _____
   💭 _____
   ◈ _____

Today, I choose to hold myself to my highest and greatest, pointed in the direction of my vision of heaven on Earth.

I upgrade my current state to...

   🔥 _____
   ⚛ _____
   🧍 _____
   💭 _____
   ◈ _____

Today, I am...

The following core
values and emotions
will support my
greatness

I choose to immediately adopt the following belief upgrades:

Belief	Upgraded Belief

As my day flows in harmony, I will...

- ☐
- ☐
- ☐
- ☐
- ☐

My gifts that will aid in the fulfilment of those goals are...

NOTES:

TITLE _____

DAY   _____

My current state is...

- _____
- _____
- _____
- _____
- _____

Today, I choose to hold myself to my highest and greatest, pointed in the direction of my vision of heaven on Earth.

I upgrade my current state to...

- _____
- _____
- _____
- _____
- _____

Today, I am...

The following core values and emotions will support my greatness

I choose to immediately adopt the following belief upgrades:

Belief	Upgraded Belief

As my day flows in harmony, I will...

☐
☐
☐
☐
☐

My gifts that will aid in the fulfilment of those goals are...

NOTES:

TITLE _____

DAY   _____

My current state is…

❦ _____
✿ _____
✝ _____
☁ _____
◈ _____

Today, I choose to hold myself to my highest and greatest, pointed in the direction of my vision of heaven on Earth.

I upgrade my current state to…

❦ _____
✿ _____
✝ _____
☁ _____
◈ _____

Today, I am...

The following core
values and emotions
will support my
greatness

I choose to immediately adopt the following belief upgrades:

Belief	Upgraded Belief

As my day flows in harmony, I will...

- ☐
- ☐
- ☐
- ☐
- ☐

My gifts that will aid in the fulfilment of those goals are...

_____

_____

_____

NOTES:

TITLE _____

DAY   _____

My current state is…

◔ ···
❀ ···
⚛ ···
☁ ···
◈ ···

Today, I choose to hold myself to my highest and greatest, pointed in the direction of my vision of heaven on Earth.

I upgrade my current state to…

◔ ···
❀ ···
⚛ ···
☁ ···
◈ ···

Today, I am...

The following core
values and emotions
will support my
greatness

I choose to immediately adopt the following belief upgrades:

Belief	Upgraded Belief

As my day flows in harmony, I will...

☐
☐
☐
☐
☐

My gifts that will aid in the fulfilment of those goals are...

NOTES:

TITLE _____

DAY   _____

My current state is…

⬥ ....
❀ ....
𝝹 ....
🗩 ....
◈ ....

Today, I choose to hold myself to my highest and greatest, pointed in the direction of my vision of heaven on Earth.

I upgrade my current state to…

⬥ ....
❀ ....
𝝹 ....
🗩 ....
◈ ....

Today, I am...

The following core
values and emotions
will support my
greatness

I choose to immediately adopt the following belief upgrades:

Belief	Upgraded Belief

As my day flows in harmony, I will...

☐
☐
☐
☐
☐

My gifts that will aid in the fulfilment of those goals are...

NOTES:

TITLE _____

DAY   _____

My current state is...

🔥 ....
❀ ....
🧍 ....
💭 ....
◈ ....

Today, I choose to hold myself to my highest and greatest, pointed in the direction of my vision of heaven on Earth.

I upgrade my current state to...

🔥 ....
❀ ....
🧍 ....
💭 ....
◈ ....

Today, I am...

The following core
values and emotions
will support my
greatness

TITLE _____

DAY _____

My current state is...

☉ _____
❀ _____
✝ _____
♡ _____
◈ _____

Today, I choose to hold myself to my highest and greatest, pointed in the direction of my vision of heaven on Earth.

I upgrade my current state to...

☉ _____
❀ _____
✝ _____
♡ _____
◈ _____

Today, I am...

The following core
values and emotions
will support my
greatness

I choose to immediately adopt the following belief upgrades:

Belief	Upgraded Belief

As my day flows in harmony, I will...

☐

☐

☐

☐

☐

My gifts that will aid in the fulfilment of those goals are...

NOTES:

I choose to immediately adopt the following belief upgrades:

Belief	Upgraded Belief

As my day flows in harmony, I will...

- ☐
- ☐
- ☐
- ☐
- ☐

My gifts that will aid in the fulfilment of those goals are...

NOTES:

TITLE _____

DAY   _____

My current state is...

🜂 _____
❀ _____
🏃 _____
💭 _____
◈ _____

Today, I choose to hold myself to my highest and greatest, pointed in the direction of my vision of heaven on Earth.

I upgrade my current state to...

🜂 _____
❀ _____
🏃 _____
💭 _____
◈ _____

Today, I am...

The following core values and emotions will support my greatness

I choose to immediately adopt the following belief upgrades:

Belief	Upgraded Belief

As my day flows in harmony, I will...

☐

☐

☐

☐

☐

My gifts that will aid in the fulfilment of those goals are...

NOTES:

TITLE _____

DAY _____

My current state is...

◊ ....
❀ ....
☥ ....
♡ ....
◈ ....

Today, I choose to hold myself to my highest and greatest, pointed in the direction of my vision of heaven on Earth.

I upgrade my current state to...

◊ ....
❀ ....
☥ ....
♡ ....
◈ ....

Today, I am...

The following core
values and emotions
will support my
greatness

I choose to immediately adopt the following belief upgrades:

Belief	Upgraded Belief

As my day flows in harmony, I will...

- ☐
- ☐
- ☐
- ☐
- ☐

My gifts that will aid in the fulfilment of those goals are...

NOTES:

TITLE ______________________

DAY ______________

My current state is...

Today, I choose to hold myself to my highest and greatest, pointed in the direction of my vision of heaven on Earth.

I upgrade my current state to...

Today, I am...

The following core values and emotions will support my greatness

I choose to immediately adopt the following belief upgrades:

Belief	Upgraded Belief

As my day flows in harmony, I will...

- ☐
- ☐
- ☐
- ☐
- ☐

My gifts that will aid in the fulfilment of those goals are...

NOTES:

TITLE _____

DAY _____

My current state is...

⚬   ....
❀   ....
🜨   ....
☁   ....
◈   ....

Today, I choose to hold myself to my highest and greatest, pointed in the direction of my vision of heaven on Earth.

I upgrade my current state to...

⚬   ....
❀   ....
🜨   ....
☁   ....
◈   ....

Today, I am...

The following core
values and emotions
will support my
greatness

I choose to immediately adopt the following belief upgrades:

Belief	Upgraded Belief

As my day flows in harmony, I will...

☐
☐
☐
☐
☐

My gifts that will aid in the fulfilment of those goals are...

NOTES:

TITLE _____

DAY   _____

My current state is...

🜂 ....
❀ ....
🜊 ....
🗩 ....
◈ ....

Today, I choose to hold myself to my highest and greatest, pointed in the direction of my vision of heaven on Earth.

I upgrade my current state to...

🜂 ....
❀ ....
🜊 ....
🗩 ....
◈ ....

Today, I am...

The following core
values and emotions
will support my
greatness

I choose to immediately adopt the following belief upgrades:

Belief	Upgraded Belief

As my day flows in harmony, I will...

☐
☐
☐
☐
☐

My gifts that will aid in the fulfilment of those goals are...

NOTES:

TITLE _____

DAY   _____

My current state is...

🔥 ....

❀ ....

👤 ....

💭 ....

◈ ....

Today, I choose to hold myself to my highest and greatest, pointed in the direction of my vision of heaven on Earth.

I upgrade my current state to...

🔥 ....

❀ ....

👤 ....

💭 ....

◈ ....

Today, I am...

The following core
values and emotions
will support my
greatness

I choose to immediately adopt the following belief upgrades:

Belief	Upgraded Belief

As my day flows in harmony, I will...

- ☐
- ☐
- ☐
- ☐
- ☐

My gifts that will aid in the fulfilment of those goals are...

NOTES:

TITLE _____

DAY   _____

My current state is...

🔥 ···
❀ ···
🕴 ···
💬 ···
◈ ···

Today, I choose to hold myself to my highest and greatest, pointed in the direction of my vision of heaven on Earth.

I upgrade my current state to...

🔥 ···
❀ ···
🕴 ···
💬 ···
◈ ···

Today, I am...

The following core
values and emotions
will support my
greatness

I choose to immediately adopt the following belief upgrades:

Belief	Upgraded Belief

As my day flows in harmony, I will...

- ☐
- ☐
- ☐
- ☐
- ☐

My gifts that will aid in the fulfilment of those goals are...

NOTES:

TITLE _____

DAY   _____

My current state is...

🔥 ....
❂ ....
🧍 ....
💬 ....
◈ ....

Today, I choose to hold myself to my highest and greatest, pointed in the direction of my vision of heaven on Earth.

I upgrade my current state to...

🔥 ....
❂ ....
🧍 ....
💬 ....
◈ ....

Today, I am...

The following core
values and emotions
will support my
greatness

I choose to immediately adopt the following belief upgrades:

Belief	Upgraded Belief

As my day flows in harmony, I will...

- ☐
- ☐
- ☐
- ☐
- ☐

My gifts that will aid in the fulfilment of those goals are...

NOTES:

TITLE _____

DAY _____

My current state is...

◉ ....
❀ ....
✝ ....
◌ ....
◈ ....

Today, I choose to hold myself to my highest and greatest, pointed in the direction of my vision of heaven on Earth.

I upgrade my current state to...

◉ ....
❀ ....
✝ ....
◌ ....
◈ ....

Today, I am...

The following core
values and emotions
will support my
greatness

I choose to immediately adopt the following belief upgrades:

Belief	Upgraded Belief

As my day flows in harmony, I will...

☐
☐
☐
☐
☐

My gifts that will aid in the fulfilment of those goals are...

NOTES:

TITLE _____

DAY   _____

My current state is…

◍ ....
❀ ....
🜨 ....
☁ ....
◈ ....

Today, I choose to hold myself to my highest and greatest, pointed in the direction of my vision of heaven on Earth.

I upgrade my current state to…

◍ ....
❀ ....
🜨 ....
☁ ....
◈ ....

Today, I am...

The following core
values and emotions
will support my
greatness

I choose to immediately adopt the following belief upgrades:

Belief	Upgraded Belief

As my day flows in harmony, I will...

- ☐
- ☐
- ☐
- ☐
- ☐

My gifts that will aid in the fulfilment of those goals are...

NOTES:

TITLE _____

DAY _____

My current state is...

◉ ....
✿ ....
🕴 ....
🗨 ....
◈ ....

Today, I choose to hold myself to my highest and greatest, pointed in the direction of my vision of heaven on Earth.

I upgrade my current state to...

◉ ....
✿ ....
🕴 ....
🗨 ....
◈ ....

Today, I am...

The following core
values and emotions
will support my
greatness

I choose to immediately adopt the following belief upgrades:

Belief	Upgraded Belief

As my day flows in harmony, I will...

☐
☐
☐
☐
☐

My gifts that will aid in the fulfilment of those goals are...

NOTES:

TITLE _____

DAY   _____

My current state is...

◉ ···
✿ ···
🕈 ···
◌ ···
◈ ···

Today, I choose to hold myself to my highest and greatest, pointed in the direction of my vision of heaven on Earth.

I upgrade my current state to...

◉ ···
✿ ···
🕈 ···
◌ ···
◈ ···

Today, I am...

The following core
values and emotions
will support my
greatness

I choose to immediately adopt the following belief upgrades:

Belief	Upgraded Belief

As my day flows in harmony, I will...

☐
☐
☐
☐
☐

My gifts that will aid in the fulfilment of those goals are...

NOTES:

TITLE _____

DAY _____

My current state is...

🔥 ....
❀ ....
👤 ....
💬 ....
◈ ....

Today, I choose to hold myself to my highest and greatest, pointed in the direction of my vision of heaven on Earth.

I upgrade my current state to...

🔥 ....
❀ ....
👤 ....
💬 ....
◈ ....

Today, I am...

The following core
values and emotions
will support my
greatness

I choose to immediately adopt the following belief upgrades:

Belief	Upgraded Belief

As my day flows in harmony, I will...

- ☐
- ☐
- ☐
- ☐
- ☐

My gifts that will aid in the fulfilment of those goals are...

NOTES:

TITLE _____

DAY   _____

My current state is…

🜂 ....
✿ ....
🜨 ....
🗨 ....
◈ ....

Today, I choose to hold myself to my highest and greatest, pointed in the direction of my vision of heaven on Earth.

I upgrade my current state to…

🜂 ....
✿ ....
🜨 ....
🗨 ....
◈ ....

Today, I am...

The following core
values and emotions
will support my
greatness

I choose to immediately adopt the following belief upgrades:

Belief	Upgraded Belief

As my day flows in harmony, I will...

- ☐
- ☐
- ☐
- ☐
- ☐

My gifts that will aid in the fulfilment of those goals are...

NOTES:

TITLE _____

DAY   _____

My current state is...

🔥 ....
⚛ ....
⚘ ....
☂ ....
◈ ....

Today, I choose to hold myself to my highest and greatest, pointed in the direction of my vision of heaven on Earth.

I upgrade my current state to...

🔥 ....
⚛ ....
⚘ ....
☂ ....
◈ ....

Today, I am...

The following core
values and emotions
will support my
greatness

I choose to immediately adopt the following belief upgrades:

Belief	Upgraded Belief

As my day flows in harmony, I will...

- ☐
- ☐
- ☐
- ☐
- ☐

My gifts that will aid in the fulfilment of those goals are...

NOTES:

TITLE _____

DAY   _____

My current state is…

⚬ ....
❀ ....
🕇 ....
💬 ....
◈ ....

Today, I choose to hold myself to my highest and greatest, pointed in the direction of my vision of heaven on Earth.

I upgrade my current state to…

⚬ ....
❀ ....
🕇 ....
💬 ....
◈ ....

Today, I am...

The following core
values and emotions
will support my
greatness

I choose to immediately adopt the following belief upgrades:

Belief	Upgraded Belief

As my day flows in harmony, I will...

☐
☐
☐
☐
☐

My gifts that will aid in the fulfilment of those goals are...

NOTES:

TITLE _____

DAY _____

My current state is...

◍ _____
❀ _____
𝕏 _____
♡ _____
◈ _____

Today, I choose to hold myself to my highest and greatest, pointed in the direction of my vision of heaven on Earth.

I upgrade my current state to...

◍ _____
❀ _____
𝕏 _____
♡ _____
◈ _____

Today, I am...

The following core
values and emotions
will support my
greatness

I choose to immediately adopt the following belief upgrades:

Belief	Upgraded Belief

As my day flows in harmony, I will...

- ☐
- ☐
- ☐
- ☐
- ☐

My gifts that will aid in the fulfilment of those goals are...

NOTES:

TITLE _____

DAY   _____

My current state is...

◍ ....
✿ ....
⍭ ....
☁ ....
◈ ....

Today, I choose to hold myself to my highest and greatest,
pointed in the direction of my vision of heaven on Earth.

I upgrade my current state to...

◍ ....
✿ ....
⍭ ....
☁ ....
◈ ....

Today, I am...

The following core
values and emotions
will support my
greatness

I choose to immediately adopt the following belief upgrades:

Belief	Upgraded Belief

As my day flows in harmony, I will...

- ☐
- ☐
- ☐
- ☐
- ☐

My gifts that will aid in the fulfilment of those goals are...

NOTES:

TITLE _____

DAY _____

My current state is...

◊ _____
❀ _____
𝞧 _____
♡ _____
◈ _____

Today, I choose to hold myself to my highest and greatest, pointed in the direction of my vision of heaven on Earth.

I upgrade my current state to...

◊ _____
❀ _____
𝞧 _____
♡ _____
◈ _____

Today, I am...

The following core
values and emotions
will support my
greatness

I choose to immediately adopt the following belief upgrades:

Belief	Upgraded Belief

As my day flows in harmony, I will...

☐

☐

☐

☐

☐

My gifts that will aid in the fulfilment of those goals are...

NOTES:

TITLE _____

DAY   _____

My current state is...

- _____
- _____
- _____
- _____
- _____

Today, I choose to hold myself to my highest and greatest, pointed in the direction of my vision of heaven on Earth.

I upgrade my current state to...

- _____
- _____
- _____
- _____
- _____

Today, I am...

The following core
values and emotions
will support my
greatness

I choose to immediately adopt the following belief upgrades:

Belief	Upgraded Belief

As my day flows in harmony, I will...

- ☐
- ☐
- ☐
- ☐
- ☐

My gifts that will aid in the fulfilment of those goals are...

NOTES:

TITLE _____

DAY   _____

My current state is...

◗ _____

✿ _____

🕆 _____

💭 _____

◈ _____

Today, I choose to hold myself to my highest and greatest, pointed in the direction of my vision of heaven on Earth.

I upgrade my current state to...

◗ _____

✿ _____

🕆 _____

💭 _____

◈ _____

Today, I am...

The following core values and emotions will support my greatness

I choose to immediately adopt the following belief upgrades:

Belief	Upgraded Belief

As my day flows in harmony, I will...

☐
☐
☐
☐
☐

My gifts that will aid in the fulfilment of those goals are...

NOTES:

TITLE _____

DAY   _____

My current state is…

🔥 _____
✿ _____
🕴 _____
💬 _____
◈ _____

Today, I choose to hold myself to my highest and greatest, pointed in the direction of my vision of heaven on Earth.

I upgrade my current state to…

🔥 _____
✿ _____
🕴 _____
💬 _____
◈ _____

Today, I am…

The following core
values and emotions
will support my
greatness

I choose to immediately adopt the following belief upgrades:

Belief	Upgraded Belief

As my day flows in harmony, I will...

- ☐
- ☐
- ☐
- ☐
- ☐

My gifts that will aid in the fulfilment of those goals are...

NOTES:

TITLE _____

DAY   _____

My current state is…

🜍 ....

✿ ....

🜨 ....

💬 ....

◈ ....

Today, I choose to hold myself to my highest and greatest, pointed in the direction of my vision of heaven on Earth.

I upgrade my current state to…

🜍 ....

✿ ....

🜨 ....

💬 ....

◈ ....

Today, I am...

The following core
values and emotions
will support my
greatness

I choose to immediately adopt the following belief upgrades:

Belief	Upgraded Belief

As my day flows in harmony, I will...

☐
☐
☐
☐
☐

My gifts that will aid in the fulfilment of those goals are...

NOTES:

TITLE _____

DAY   _____

My current state is...

◊ ....

✿ ....

大 ....

♡ ....

◈ ....

Today, I choose to hold myself to my highest and greatest, pointed in the direction of my vision of heaven on Earth.

I upgrade my current state to...

◊ ....

✿ ....

大 ....

♡ ....

◈ ....

Today, I am...

The following core
values and emotions
will support my
greatness

I choose to immediately adopt the following belief upgrades:

Belief	Upgraded Belief

As my day flows in harmony, I will...

- ☐
- ☐
- ☐
- ☐
- ☐

My gifts that will aid in the fulfilment of those goals are...

NOTES:

TITLE _____

DAY   _____

My current state is...

�उ   ....
❀   ....
⚘   ....
○   ....
◈   ....

Today, I choose to hold myself to my highest and greatest, pointed in the direction of my vision of heaven on Earth.

I upgrade my current state to...

◑   ....
❀   ....
⚘   ....
○   ....
◈   ....

Today, I am...

The following core
values and emotions
will support my
greatness

I choose to immediately adopt the following belief upgrades:

Belief	Upgraded Belief

As my day flows in harmony, I will...

- ☐
- ☐
- ☐
- ☐
- ☐

My gifts that will aid in the fulfilment of those goals are...

NOTES:

TITLE _____

DAY   _____

My current state is...

◖ ....
✿ ....
ㅈ ....
◌ ....
◈ ....

Today, I choose to hold myself to my highest and greatest, pointed in the direction of my vision of heaven on Earth.

I upgrade my current state to...

◖ ....
✿ ....
ㅈ ....
◌ ....
◈ ....

Today, I am...

The following core
values and emotions
will support my
greatness

I choose to immediately adopt the following belief upgrades:

Belief	Upgraded Belief

As my day flows in harmony, I will...

- ☐
- ☐
- ☐
- ☐
- ☐

My gifts that will aid in the fulfilment of those goals are...

NOTES:

TITLE _____

DAY   _____

My current state is…

🔥 ....
❀ ....
𝈐 ....
☁ ....
◈ ....

Today, I choose to hold myself to my highest and greatest, pointed in the direction of my vision of heaven on Earth.

I upgrade my current state to…

🔥 ....
❀ ....
𝈐 ....
☁ ....
◈ ....

Today, I am...

The following core
values and emotions
will support my
greatness

I choose to immediately adopt the following belief upgrades:

Belief	Upgraded Belief

As my day flows in harmony, I will...

☐
☐
☐
☐
☐

My gifts that will aid in the fulfilment of those goals are...

NOTES:

TITLE _____

DAY _____

My current state is...

◊ _____
❀ _____
✝ _____
○ _____
◈ _____

Today, I choose to hold myself to my highest and greatest, pointed in the direction of my vision of heaven on Earth.

I upgrade my current state to...

◊ _____
❀ _____
✝ _____
○ _____
◈ _____

Today, I am...

The following core values and emotions will support my greatness

I choose to immediately adopt the following belief upgrades:

Belief	Upgraded Belief

As my day flows in harmony, I will...

- ☐
- ☐
- ☐
- ☐
- ☐

My gifts that will aid in the fulfilment of those goals are...

_____

_____

NOTES:

TITLE _____

DAY _____

My current state is...

◔
✿
⚘
♡
◈ _____

Today, I choose to hold myself to my highest and greatest, pointed in the direction of my vision of heaven on Earth.

I upgrade my current state to...

◔
✿
⚘
♡
◈

Today, I am...

The following core
values and emotions
will support my
greatness

I choose to immediately adopt the following belief upgrades:

Belief	Upgraded Belief

As my day flows in harmony, I will...

☐
☐
☐
☐
☐

My gifts that will aid in the fulfilment of those goals are...

NOTES:

TITLE _____

DAY   _____

My current state is...

🔥 _____

✿ _____

🧍 _____

🗩 _____

◈ _____

Today, I choose to hold myself to my highest and greatest, pointed in the direction of my vision of heaven on Earth.

I upgrade my current state to...

🔥 _____

✿ _____

🧍 _____

🗩 _____

◈ _____

Today, I am...

The following core
values and emotions
will support my
greatness

I choose to immediately adopt the following belief upgrades:

Belief	Upgraded Belief

As my day flows in harmony, I will...

- [ ]
- [ ]
- [ ]
- [ ]
- [ ]

My gifts that will aid in the fulfilment of those goals are...

NOTES:

TITLE _____

DAY _____

My current state is...

🜂 ....
❀ ....
🕴 ....
💭 ....
◈ ....

Today, I choose to hold myself to my highest and greatest, pointed in the direction of my vision of heaven on Earth.

I upgrade my current state to...

🜂 ....
❀ ....
🕴 ....
💭 ....
◈ ....

Today, I am...

The following core
values and emotions
will support my
greatness

I choose to immediately adopt the following belief upgrades:

Belief	Upgraded Belief

As my day flows in harmony, I will...

☐
☐
☐
☐
☐

My gifts that will aid in the fulfilment of those goals are...

NOTES:

TITLE _____

DAY   _____

My current state is...

◑ ....
❀ ....
大 ....
♡ ....
◈ ....

Today, I choose to hold myself to my highest and greatest, pointed in the direction of my vision of heaven on Earth.

I upgrade my current state to...

◑ ....
❀ ....
大 ....
♡ ....
◈ ....

Today, I am...

The following core
values and emotions
will support my
greatness

I choose to immediately adopt the following belief upgrades:

Belief	Upgraded Belief

As my day flows in harmony, I will...

- ☐
- ☐
- ☐
- ☐
- ☐

My gifts that will aid in the fulfilment of those goals are...

NOTES:

TITLE _____

DAY   _____

My current state is...

◐ ....
❀ ....
🕴 ....
💬 ....
◈ ....

Today, I choose to hold myself to my highest and greatest, pointed in the direction of my vision of heaven on Earth.

I upgrade my current state to...

◐ ....
❀ ....
🕴 ....
💬 ....
◈ ....

Today, I am...

The following core values and emotions will support my greatness

I choose to immediately adopt the following belief upgrades:

Belief	Upgraded Belief

As my day flows in harmony, I will...

- ☐
- ☐
- ☐
- ☐
- ☐

My gifts that will aid in the fulfilment of those goals are...

NOTES:

TITLE _____

DAY   _____

My current state is…

◐ ....
❀ ....
⼓ ....
◌ ....
◈ ....

Today, I choose to hold myself to my highest and greatest, pointed in the direction of my vision of heaven on Earth.

I upgrade my current state to…

◐ ....
❀ ....
⼓ ....
◌ ....
◈ ....

Today, I am...

The following core values and emotions will support my greatness			

I choose to immediately adopt the following belief upgrades:

Belief	Upgraded Belief

As my day flows in harmony, I will...

☐
☐
☐
☐
☐

My gifts that will aid in the fulfilment of those goals are...

NOTES:

TITLE _____

DAY   _____

My current state is...

�   ....
❀   ....
⩵   ....
☁   ....
◈   ....

Today, I choose to hold myself to my highest and greatest, pointed in the direction of my vision of heaven on Earth.

I upgrade my current state to...

◵   ....
❀   ....
⩵   ....
☁   ....
◈   ....

Today, I am...

The following core
values and emotions
will support my
greatness

I choose to immediately adopt the following belief upgrades:

Belief	Upgraded Belief

As my day flows in harmony, I will...

- ☐
- ☐
- ☐
- ☐
- ☐

My gifts that will aid in the fulfilment of those goals are...

NOTES:

TITLE _____

DAY _____

My current state is…

◐ ....
❀ ....
✝ ....
♡ ....
◈ ....

Today, I choose to hold myself to my highest and greatest, pointed in the direction of my vision of heaven on Earth.

I upgrade my current state to…

◐ ....
❀ ....
✝ ....
♡ ....
◈ ....

Today, I am...

The following core values and emotions will support my greatness

I choose to immediately adopt the following belief upgrades:

Belief	Upgraded Belief

As my day flows in harmony, I will...

- ☐
- ☐
- ☐
- ☐
- ☐

My gifts that will aid in the fulfilment of those goals are...

NOTES:

TITLE _____

DAY _____

My current state is…

🔥 ···
🏵 ···
🕴 ···
💭 ···
◈ ···

Today, I choose to hold myself to my highest and greatest, pointed in the direction of my vision of heaven on Earth.

I upgrade my current state to…

🔥 ···
🏵 ···
🕴 ···
💭 ···
◈ ···

Today, I am...

The following core
values and emotions
will support my
greatness

I choose to immediately adopt the following belief upgrades:

Belief	Upgraded Belief

As my day flows in harmony, I will...

☐
☐
☐
☐
☐

My gifts that will aid in the fulfilment of those goals are...

NOTES:

TITLE _____

DAY _____

My current state is...

🔥 ....
⚛ ....
🕴 ....
💬 ....
◈ ....

Today, I choose to hold myself to my highest and greatest, pointed in the direction of my vision of heaven on Earth.

I upgrade my current state to...

🔥 ....
⚛ ....
🕴 ....
💬 ....
◈ ....

Today, I am...

The following core
values and emotions
will support my
greatness

I choose to immediately adopt the following belief upgrades:

Belief	Upgraded Belief

As my day flows in harmony, I will...

☐

☐

☐

☐

☐

My gifts that will aid in the fulfilment of those goals are...

NOTES:

TITLE _____

DAY   _____

My current state is…

🔥 ....
❀ ....
🕴 ....
💬 ....
◈ ....

Today, I choose to hold myself to my highest and greatest, pointed in the direction of my vision of heaven on Earth.

I upgrade my current state to…

🔥 ....
❀ ....
🕴 ....
💬 ....
◈ ....

Today, I am...

The following core
values and emotions
will support my
greatness

I choose to immediately adopt the following belief upgrades:

Belief	Upgraded Belief

As my day flows in harmony, I will...

- ☐
- ☐
- ☐
- ☐
- ☐

My gifts that will aid in the fulfilment of those goals are...

NOTES:

TITLE _____

DAY   _____

My current state is…

�
❀
🕇
◯
◈
_____

Today, I choose to hold myself to my highest and greatest, pointed in the direction of my vision of heaven on Earth.

I upgrade my current state to…

◍
❀
🕇
◯
◈

Today, I am...

The following core values and emotions will support my greatness

I choose to immediately adopt the following belief upgrades:

Belief	Upgraded Belief

As my day flows in harmony, I will...

☐
☐
☐
☐
☐

My gifts that will aid in the fulfilment of those goals are...

NOTES:

TITLE   _____

DAY   _____

My current state is...

🔥   _____

✿   _____

🕴   _____

💭   _____

◈   _____

Today, I choose to hold myself to my highest and greatest, pointed in the direction of my vision of heaven on Earth.

I upgrade my current state to...

🔥   _____

✿   _____

🕴   _____

💭   _____

◈   _____

Today, I am...

The following core
values and emotions
will support my
greatness

I choose to immediately adopt the following belief upgrades:

Belief	Upgraded Belief

As my day flows in harmony, I will...

- ☐
- ☐
- ☐
- ☐
- ☐

My gifts that will aid in the fulfilment of those goals are...

NOTES:

TITLE _____

DAY

                        _____

My current state is...

🔥 _____

⚘ _____

🚶 _____

☁ _____

❖ _____

Today, I choose to hold myself to my highest and greatest, pointed in the direction of my vision of heaven on Earth.

I upgrade my current state to...

🔥 _____

⚘ _____

🚶 _____

☁ _____

❖ _____

Today, I am...

The following core
values and emotions
will support my
greatness

I choose to immediately adopt the following belief upgrades:

Belief	Upgraded Belief

As my day flows in harmony, I will...

- ☐
- ☐
- ☐
- ☐
- ☐

My gifts that will aid in the fulfilment of those goals are...

NOTES:

TITLE _____

DAY   _____

My current state is...

�434 _____
❀ _____
🕇 _____
💭 _____
◈ _____

Today, I choose to hold myself to my highest and greatest, pointed in the direction of my vision of heaven on Earth.

I upgrade my current state to...

�434 _____
❀ _____
🕇 _____
💭 _____
◈ _____

Today, I am...

The following core values and emotions will support my greatness			

I choose to immediately adopt the following belief upgrades:

Belief	Upgraded Belief

As my day flows in harmony, I will...

☐
☐
☐
☐
☐

My gifts that will aid in the fulfilment of those goals are...

NOTES:

www.ingramcontent.com/pod-product-compliance
Lightning Source LLC
Chambersburg PA
CBHW022006090426
42741CB00007B/920